Basic Programming and Problem Solving

Kyle Langley

About the Author

Kyle Langley is a self-taught game designer who has worked on games such as *Transformers: Fall of Cybertron* released by High Moon Studios and *Warm Gun, Carnival of Bullets*, and *Maximum Overdrive* released by Emotional Robots. He is currently developing a multi-player PC title for Vex Studios called *Jeklynn Heights*. Kyle has also tutored many game design students and has previously released two beginners' programming books. The first for Unreal Development Kit called *Learn Programming With Unreal Script*. The second called *Learn Unity iOS Game Development*. His website is, **www.dotvawxgames.com.**

Thanks to Courtney Phillips for the support and advice.

Table of Contents

Introduction

Chances are that if you picked up this book you are either starting to learn how to program or are interested in it. My goal is to explain what I have learned with my study of programming and give you an insight in the areas that I found confusing.

A few things I won't do:

- Tell you that you have to learn or use any one facet of the programming world. This includes but is not limited to languages, frameworks, libraries, or methodologies.
- Promote any piece of software or computer hardware. Laptop, desktop, Mac, Linux, or Windows will suite you just fine.
- Try to convince you of the "right" way to program.
- Dive into big portions of computer science. I will touch some of it though so you get an understanding of what is going at the lower level.

Things I will try to do:

- Give you some sort of reason to what I am explaining, with the pros and cons I have come across doing said thing.
- Give you options so you can have the information to explore on your own. I don't want to put you into a box and hope you find your way out.
- Break down all explanations and simply as I can.

There will be some formatting options to aid you throughout the book. They are as follows:

italics will represent any piece of code from the problem. It will be a way for you to look back at the code to see what I am referencing when I am explaining what it does.

What is programming?

The process in which modern computers work started with Alan Turing, who most notably helped the Allies break German ciphers during World War Two. Turing wrote a paper called, *Computing Machinery and Intelligence* which at its time was a hypothetical way to use a single machine to solve any sort of computation. His paper lead us into the modern computing age using the principle of reading individual bytes and choosing to act on, change, or if the byte is empty, ignore it. This is exactly how ram works today.

Learning to write code is a way for you to give a higher level instruction which at a certain point, will be converted into these bytes, represented by 0 and 1, often refereed to as binary code. Processors have a huge amount of power and read what is called, machine code or referred to by the language name, Assembly. Assembly is the lowest level programming language which can be read by humans, realistically. Processors also have code embedded on them to help with certain common routines which makes those computations faster.

Programming is full of higher level languages that give you a platform that does almost all lower level functions for you, usually at the cost of performance. As an example, lets say you work with a language that manages memory. What if this language manages memory in a way that is not efficient for you program? This is often the trade of you have to accept. Now, depending on what you are doing, this is a perfectly acceptable trade off but not knowing what these languages do at these levels is often why some software is slow. When's the last time you opened up something like a text editor and it took 10-20 seconds to open? This is often the sort of result of code that is not optimized.

While all this is a bit out of scope of what you'll be learning in this book, I want you to know that if you are interested in the future, you can learn to do these things yourself and create software that will run more efficiently that letting predefined code do some of that heavy lifting for you.

The practice of programming

Before I get started with anything else, I want to explain the process of what it is to write a computer program.

I think of it as an approach in which I get to solve the problems I have created in order to accomplish a bigger task(s) of having a computer do something I want. Software is made up of thousands of individual problems. The solution to each one of these problems will lead a through the program, achieving the final result the program was designed for.

As an example, a simple program might allow the user to take down a note and then open it up again later. At a basic level, this program has a handful of problems that need to be solved in order for it to work.

This could be a starting outline:

* The program opens and closes when the user wants it to. The program has a "main" loop, which keeps the programming running until the user tells it not to.
* The program has a visual element for the user to see. Graphical code has to be written or used.
* The user can change the visual elements to navigate through the program. Some graphics need to be interactive, such as a button.
* The user can input some sort of text into a visual element. The program needs to take events from an input device, such as a keyboard, and display them in a visual element.
* The user can save this input with a visual element. The program needs to take an event that will trigger another event to store this text in some sort of file on the hard drive of their device.
* The user can see all the saved inputs from previous saves. The program needs to be able to load the file saved and read from it.
* The user can delete an individual input from the list of saves. The program needs to be able to delete a file without destroying the rest of the saved items.

There are thousands of tools and libraries that you could use so this type of program could be completed in a matter of minutes, once you get the hang of things. It is pretty rare for a programmer to not use any of these tools or libraries. But as you can see, there is still a rational and linear approach to writing a computer program. One of the things I've noticed is many beginners will get overwhelmed and try to do two things at once. If you are ever feeling over whelmed, take a step back for a second and think about what would be better; can you break this into more than one problem or can you make it more simple?

Programming languages

There are a lot of programming languages in the world. Many are used for individual projects, others are general purpose languages that offer you the luxury of using them for just about anything you'd like. When learning, it is common to choose a higher level language that does a portion of the heavy lifting for you; such as managing memory or including some inherent function, like string manipulation. These types of languages are refereed to as managed languages. Some examples are Java Script, Ruby, C#, and Java.

The difference of most languages is simply syntax. While there are also some minor differences in structure, learning syntactical changes between them will often let you switch between languages once you have figured out the basic sort of logic behind programming as a whole.

For the purposes of this book, I will try not to use any one language but instead give you some example in different languages so you can both see the similarities and allow you to follow along. My goal here is to teach how to break down a variety of the technical problems you may face and transition them into code.

The three languages the book will use are:

- JavaScript
- Ruby
- C#

I have picked these three because they offer a variety between web, scripting, and software development.

Programming culture

Academia has a big effect on programming. So much so that it is not uncommon for an instructional book to be written and even critically acclaimed by an author who hasn't written a single piece of software in years. It is the type of learning resource that gives a very precise and technical view of a programming language without much resource for practical use. This type of education leads to a hardened approach to how to write a computer program. This is where you may hear of a programmer explaining why his or her method is the best way to do it. I want you to do your best to find your way. Programming is a practice with many tools. To ignore a chunk of them based on the mentality that one way is better than another will not do you any favors. The truth is that some languages are better than others for specific things; what these things are varies from language to language and it's up to the programmers to figure out what that is and why they should use it.

Now, with that said. This topic is heavily debated and criticized by the industry. People and companies in it have a method and they follow it for business and organizational reasons. This means that if you get to the point of getting hired at a studio, company, or other type of business that wants you to program for them, you will probably have to follow the way they want you to do it, regardless if it goes against what you believe or even what you know is inefficient or simply a bad practice.

What I would like most from you is to keep an open mind and enjoy programming. What you discover about it and what you would like to follow is up to you. I try to be like the scientists in the world: understand as much as you can but if you discover something new, don't ignore it. Let the new information change you and you will be better for it. Being stubborn makes it difficult to grow as a computer programmer.

Programming as a practice

Programming, like any skill, takes a fair bit of time to begin to understand. This is completely normal, so do not feel discouraged or that you are not performing at the pace you think you should be. The bottom line is, programming is difficult.

I look at programming as a talent with a never ending amount of study. It's one of the reasons I chose it as a career path. I feel that if you are always moving forward, you will always have a new goal to reach. This means that programming generally takes a fair bit of continual interest to keep getting better. It is difficult to stay working as a programmer if you give up on learning how programming is changing, cause it is always changing. As technology continues to grow, so does the languages behind it.

At a higher level, programming is the declaration, assignment, and manipulation of data within a program. It is your job to reference and change the data so the user is able to use the program in the way you have designed it.

For practice, I highly recommend this website: **https://codepad.remoteinterview.io**

Codepad will give you the option to use all three languages I will be using for the examples as well as many more for you to experiment with on your own.

Variables

Different programming languages have different ways of declaring a variable - variables are a way to assign a value to a name.

As an example:

```
var x = 0;
```

You can now use x and it will be displayed as the value its set to; in this case, 0;

There are many types you can assign to a variable, here is a list of some:

```
var floatingPoint    = 1.25;
var integerValue     = 3034;
var stringName       = "Hello!";
var boolBinary       = false;
var arrayList        = [1, 2, 3, 4, 5];
var object           = new MyObject( );
```

Floating Point numbers are those with a decimal point. These are used calculating problems that numerical precision.

Integer values are whole numbers. These do not have any decimal points are used when you don't need the precision between whole values.
Strings are a group of characters. These are often used for storing the text you may want to display to the end user.

Bool, or Booleans, are binary values. As in, they are either true or false. You can also think of them as 0 (false) and 1 (true);

Arrays are a container to store many of the same type with one exception, languages that are not type specific, such as JavaScript and Ruby look at arrays if a list of any type of data. In the example above, it is a container that holds 5 integer values. Elements in arrays are referenced by an index. This index starts at 0 (not 1) and continue to the size of the array - 1. This means that if an array holds 5 elements, the index values would be: 0,1,2,3,4. This is a bit confusing at first but once you get used to the idea that arrays index values start at 0, working with them becomes a bit easier.

Objects are storage for many types. As an example, you could have an object that is called Human. Humans could have variables for age, name, height, weight, race, religion, and so on. Each one of these values withing Human could then be accessed and changed.

Languages also offer you a variable that is the lack of a value. This called by many names: *null, none, nil, NilObject, undefined,* and some more. These are a way to see if a variable has any type to it, as it is possible to have a variable with no type.

You could also create a variable, such as:

```
var x;
```

Now x will have no specific value but can technically be used. Languages handle this in a few different ways, mostly by telling you that you have created a variable but haven't assigned it to anything.

In Object-Oriented programming (OOP), objects are created through what is called a class. In non OOP, they are stored in what is called a struct. Structs behave much like a class without the features in OOP. Objects are your way of storing as much data as you want through a single name. Depending on the language, you access the data in these objects by using what is called the dot operator which allows you to access these member variables.

As an example:

```
Human.age        = 29;
Human.weight     = 158.64;
Human.language   = "English";
```

Fortunately, there aren't that many to remember, the cool part is that that most programs use a variation of just these to complete their tasks.

Type declaration

Declaring variables works differently between languages, though there is some overlap.

Most of the languages you use for web development use a sort of open variable declaration. This means that variables don't have a designated type, so they can change through the course of the program; if you want them to. With that in mind, this causes some issue when developing because any variable can hold any type causing you to potentially lose track of what type you are using as the declaration of it is the same as every other variable.

For the three languages were using:

JavaScript:

```
var x = 0;
```

Ruby:

```
x = 0
```

C#:

```
int x = 0;
```

Languages like C# use designated types. Type specific variables are a bit more rigid but give you the reliability that the variable you are using will always be that type; the only caveat to this is that with inheritance (objects that extend from another or take on the data from another object) can be cast into another of the types it came from. We will get into this later.

These types could be written as:

```
float floatingPoint      = 1.25;
int number               = 3034;
string greeting          = "Hello!";
bool isTrue              = false;
int countToFive[ ]       = new int[1, 2, 3, 4, 5];
MyObject object          = new MyObject( );
```

When dealing with types, if you were to do something like:

```
int myInt;
```

This is a standard type and would probably default to a value, most likely 0. This means if you were to use myInt, it would be 0. If you were using a object with different types, there would be no default value and it would probably come back as what we talked about before; null, none, nil, NilObject, etc. This would be bad as the program wouldn't know what to do with it and depending on the language, could crash the program when trying to use it.

Control flow

A big portion of programming is guiding the program through what it should be doing based on what the values of its data are set to. Conditional statements allow you to change the way the flow of a program based on the values currently set within it.

Controlling what a program does is largely done through the following:

- Conditional Statements.
- Logical Statements.
- Arithmetic.
- Compound assignment (shorthand for arithmetic operators).
- Loops.

Conditional Operators

As an example, lets say you were checking all the Human objects in your program to see their age but you only wanted to know if they are less than 25 years old.

The condition for this would be:

```
human.age < 25
```

The general conditional operators are as follows:

Greater than:	>
Greater than or equal to:	>=
Less than:	<
Less than or equal to:	<=
Equal to:	==
NOT equal to:	!=

Here are some examples of conditions and their results:

```
4 < 3              : false
4 > 3              : true
38 >= 40           : false
38 <= 40           : true
40 >= 40           : true
38 <= 38           : true
true == true       : true
false == true      : false
false != true      : true
1.25 == 1          : false
898.342 != 898     : true
```

JavaScript has a few more with some extra rules:

Equal value but different type:	==
Equal value same type:	===
Not equal value and different type:	!=
Not equal value but same type:	!==

These have to do with checking specific types with each other, such as:

```
x = "1"
y = 1
x == y (true)
x === y (false)
```

Because x is a string and y is an integer, the == will pass because JavaScript determines the string of "1" to equal 1 as a possible conversion of the string is the integer value of 1. But, if you use === it checks to make sure that the conditional values on the left and right side are the same type, meaning if one is a string and another is an integer, it wont pass.

This is the same for the != and !== conditional operators.

```
x = "1"
y = 1
x != y  (false)
```

x and y aren't different here in JavaScript eyes because 1 can be converted to y.

```
x = "1"
y = 1
x !== y (true)
```

This on the other hand will be true because x and y are different types, so they don't equal each other with the !== conditional operator.

Logical operators

The next are ways of having multiple conditional statements in line with each other, called logical operators, and all will have to be true for the entire condition to pass:

Or: ||
And: &&

Examples of these two:

4 < 3 && 3 > 4   : false
(4 is less than 3 AND 3 is greater than 4)

1.34 > 1 && 1.15 > 1   : true
(1.34 is greater than 1 AND 1.15 is greater than 1)

34 >= 34 && 1340 < 2000   : true
(34 is greater than or equal to 34 AND 1340 is less than 2000)

4 < 3 || 12 > 4   : true
(4 is less than 3 OR 12 > 4)

12.34 != 12 || 1 != 1   : true
 (12.34 doesn't equal 12 OR 1 doesn't equal 1)

You can string these together such as:

4 < 3 && 3 > 4 && 1.34 > 1 && 1.15 > 1 || 12 > 4   : true
(4 is less than 3 AND 3 is greater than 4 AND 1.34 is greater than 1 AND 1.15 greater than 1 OR 4 less than 3 OR 12 greater than 4)

The above would evaluate to true as 12 is greater than 4 and its as a OR, meaning if its true the entire condition will be as well.

Some more abstract conditional statements happen when you start to compare to variables with each other; which you don't directly know what the value is. This could be something like:

```
humanOne.age == humanTwo.age
```

Or another example using logical operators:

```
humanOne.age == humanTwo.age && humanOne.height > humanTwo.height
```

Looking at this doesn't give you much because you don't directly know the age of *humanOne* or *humanTwo*. But, you do know why you are using the conditional. As in, if you want to see if both humans have the same age, it doesn't matter what their age is, only that it is the same.

Using these conditional and logical operators in a program is done in a few ways. The first is if which could be written like this:

JavaScript:
```
if( x > y )
{
      // Execute code here if condition is true
}
```

Ruby:
```
if x >= y
      # Execute code here if condition is true
end
```

C#:
```
if( x < y )
{
      // Execute code here if condition is true
}
```

Since there needs to be an area of code to run if these conditions run, JavaScript and C# use brackets ({ }) to designate said area. For Ruby, everything before the keyword end is what will be run if the condition is true.

Also, every language has a method in which a programmer can leave notes in the code, generally called comments. JavaScript and C# denote these with two back slashes (//) while Ruby uses a pound / hash tag (#). This code will not be run when executed, it is a way for you to put plain text into the code without worry of it messing up anything.

If any of these conditions were to evaluate to true, the code within the block of the condition would be run. As an example of this:

JavaScript:
```
if( x > y )
{
    x = y;
}
```

Ruby:
```
if x >= y
    x = y
end
```

C#:
```
if( x < y )
{
    Y = x;
}
```

These conditional statements can also be strung together with the elseif for Javascript and C# and elsif with Ruby. As an example:

JavaScript:
```
if( x > y )
{
    x = y;
}
else if( z > a )
{
    Z = a;
}
```

Ruby:
```
if x > y
    x = y
elsif z > a
    Z = a
end
```

C#:
```
if( x < y )
{
    Y = x;
}
else if( z > a )
{
    Z = a;
}
```

The keyword *else* is a way to say if no other condition is true, run the code in that block.

JavaScript:
```
if( x > y )
{
    x = y;
}
else if( z > a )
{
    z = a;
}
else
{
    b = c;
}
```

Ruby:
```
if x > y
    x = y
elsif z > a
    z = a
else
    b = c
end
```

C#:
```
if( x < y )
{
    Y = x;
}
else if( z > a )
{
    z = a;
}
else
{
    b = c;
}
```

To break this down:

If *x* is *not* greater than y check if z is greater than *a*, if that is *not true,* set *b* to be equal to *c.*

> You can have as many else if / elsif as you want but you can only have one if and one else in the conditions, if strung together as they are here.

Arithmetic operators

Standard arithmetic operators are supported universally through all programming languages. These are the same as what you're used to from all of you mathematics education.

They as follows:

+	Addition.
-	Subtraction.
*	Multiplication.
/	Division
%	Remainder after division.
++	Increment by 1.
—	Decrement by 1.
=	Assignment.

Addition (+) takes the left and right value and adds them together:

```
1 + 2 = 3
```

Subtraction (-) takes the left and right value and subtracts them from each other, left to right.

```
3 - 1 = 2
```

Multiplication (*) takes the left and right values and multiplies them.

```
3 * 4 = 12
```

Division (/) takes the left and right values and divides them.

```
24 / 3 = 8
```

Modulo (%) divides the left and right values and gives you the remainder.

```
24 % 3 = 0
25 % 3 = 1
```

Increment (++) takes the current value and adds 1 to it.

4++ = 5

Decrement(--) takes the current value and subtracts 1 from it.

5-- = 4

Assignment takes the right side expression and assigns it to the left value.

x = 5 + 4
x = 9

y = 34 - 20
y = 14

These are universal through the majority programming languages.

Operator precedence

Like traditional math, these operators have an order in which they are calculated.

The order is:

1. Increment   ++
   Decrement   –

2. Multiplication   *
   Division   /
   Modulo / remainder   %

3. Addition   +
   Subtraction   –

As an example:

x = 3 + 4 * 12

This will be calculated with 4 * 12 first, then add the result with 3 meaning X will equal 51.

Let's say you wanted to add 3 to 4 before multiplying them.

x = (3 + 4) * 12

The braces ( ) around 3 + 4 will give precedence to that calculation first, resulting in X equaling 84, as 3 + 4 is 7, times 12 is 84.
You can segregate mathematical operations in more complex ways as well:

x = ((3 + 4) * 12) * ((40 + 12) * 3)

This would first do 3 + 4, then multiply that by 12. Next, it would do 40 + 12 and multiply that by 3. Finally, it would take the result of (3 + 4) * 12 and multiply it with (40 + 12) * 3 and giving you the result. X here would be, 13104 as that is the product of 84 * 156.

Compound assignment operators

Compound assignment operators are a bit of short hand, mixing the arithmetic operators with the assignment operator.

They are as follows:

Add the left side value with right side value: +=
Subtract the left side value with right side value: -=
Divide the left side value with right side value: /=
Multiply the left side value with right side value: *=

This:

```
x = 1
x = x + 4
```
(x is now 5)

Is the same as:

```
x = 1
x += 4
```
(x = is now 5)

A more complex example:

```
FinalPrice = 0
CurrentPrice = 120
UnitsOfProduct = 4

FinalPrice += CurrentPrice * UnitsOfProduct
```
(Final price is equal to 480)

Even more complex:

```
DiscountPercent        = 0.25
Discount               = 0
FinalPrice             = 0
CurrentPrice           = 120
UnitsOfProduct         = 4

FinalPrice += CurrentPrice * UnitsOfProduct
Discount = FinalPrice * DiscountPercent
FinalPrice -= Discount
```
(Final price is equal to 360)

Functions / Methods

Methods, or more commonly known as functions, are a way for you to write a small portion of code that is for one task.

Like variables, depending on the language you are using, you will define a function in different ways. As an example, here are how a few different languages want you to write a function:

JavaScript:

```
function MyFunctionName( )
{
}
```

Ruby:

```
def myFunctionName
end
```

C#:

```
void MyFunctionName( )
{
}
```

When writing functions with Ruby, you cannot use capital letters to start the function. This is because Ruby reserves anything starting with a capital letter. JavaScript and C# don't share the same restriction.

Like variables, you can name your function anything you want, as long as it is not declared anywhere else in your program; the only exception here is that some languages allow you to have what is called function overloading. This is a way for you to have multiple functions with the same name that take in a different number of arguments, so you can use any of them in a way that you want. For the purposes of what we are trying to accomplish, we will only use one function with one name.

Function arguments are a way to send data into a function. They would be written like:

JavaScript:

```
function MyFunctionName( ArguementName )
{
}
```

Ruby:

```
def myFunctionName( argumentName )
end
```

C#:

```
void MyFunctionName( int ArgumentName )
{
}
```

It is important to remember that in these examples *ArgumentName* only exists within that function. As soon as that function is done, *ArgumentName* is no longer usable (referenced) anywhere else in code. Think of it as when you send a variable into a function, that variable is copied and used with the name of the argument instead.

Some languages, such as C#, require you to declare a type for both what the function will return and the type of the argument being passed into the function.

Passing in an argument will allow you to change it within the function and then when the function is done, it could potentially return a modified version of that argument. As an example:

C#:

```
int AddFiveTo( int Number )
{
    return Number + 5;
}
```

Other languages, such as Ruby and JavaScript do not have the requirement of typed variables or functions. You could write the same function like:

JavaScript:

```
function AddFiveTo( Number )
{
    return Number + 5;
}
```

Ruby:

```
def addFiveTo( number )
    return number + 5
end
```

Classes / Objects

The premise of Object Oriented Programming is defining and using classes to create a representation of a real world object. Many examples start with something like cars, humans, fruit, and so on. The basic idea of classes though is that they hold a re-usable sort of data where you are able to reference the data based on the name of the object they exist in. As an example:

```
myHuman.age
myFruit.sweetness
myCar.color
```

Age, *sweetness*, and *color* would all be member variables (meaning they are a part of the object they represent). Then when you create an instance (a copy) of this class, you can access and modify these individual variables for your needs through what's called the dot operator.

An important thing to remember is that OOP is rooted in the idea that most, if not all, data needs to exist within these class / objects, which can be cumbersome when dealing with projects not so rooted in the model of basing them off real world objects. This model also abstracts (hides) data within these objects in varying levels of accessibility. While not hugely important in what we will be going over, these levels are public (accessible to anything with reference to the object), protected (accessible to the object itself and any object that inherits from it), private (only accessible to this object). You will notice through the examples, only C# will be using any of these because by default, C# sets member variables to private. If at any point I use a protection level for a real reason, I will explicitly say so and tell you why.

There are all sorts of arguments for and against OOP but all you need to know is how to organize your data and use it. Later down the road, if you want to try a functional based programming language which doesn't rely on the OOP model, I suggest you start with the programming language C; not to be confused with C# or C++.

Here are some basic examples of objects:

JavaScript:

```
function Test( x, y )
{
    this.x = x;
    this.y = x;
}
```

Ruby:

```
class Test
    attr_reader :x, :y
    def initialize( x, y )
        @x = x
        @y = y
    end
end
```

C#:

```
public class Test
{
    public int x;
    public int y;

    public Test( int x, int y )
    {
        this.x = x;
        this.y = y;
    }
}
```

Generally speaking, you need to create an instance of an object to access the member variables within in. This is done by:

JavaScript:

```
var testObject = new Test( 3, 4 );

(testObject.x = 3)
(testObject.y = 4)
```

Ruby:

```
testObject = Test.new( 13, 14 )

(testObject.x = 13)
(testObject.y = 14)
```

C#:

```
Test testObject = new Test( 23, 12 );

(testObject.x = 23)
(testObject.y = 12)
```

testObject in all three cases here is the variable name with the type of Test. Each one of these objects have an initializer (also called a constructor) where you can pass in the two values you want to use for x and y. With *testObject* created, you know have an instance of the class as an object and can manipulate the member variables within it anyway you see fit.

You'll notice that in JavaScript the *testObject* variable needs to have var in front if it. This is like what we went over in the variables chapter where in order to keep a reference to the object instance, you need to define the variable with a name and then assign a reference to it; in this case, the class of Test will become the object of *testObject*.

In Ruby, you do not need to define the type of the variable. Ruby assumes any unique name will be a variable and the type of that variable is set when it is assigned. In our case, *testObject* will be assigned to the Test class/object.

In C#, you have to declare the type of the variable before assigning it, which is why Test is before the variable name *testObject*. This means that *testObject* will be the type of Test. Just like before in the variables chapter where you had to give C# variables the type of int, string, bool, etc, when dealing with object instances, you have to give that variable the type of the class for the object instance.

Another important thing to remember is that when that both JavaScript and C# require a semicolon(;) at the end of your lines of code. This a sign for the compiler to know when a line of code ends and when the next one starts. JavaScript is a bit lenient on this and there are some fail safes in many modern web browsers to assume when lines of code end but it is still a good thing to do. Ruby does not have this requirement and when a block needs to end, Ruby uses the keyword end. This practice will be more apparent when we start the practice problems.

Static Classes

Static classes are a way to have a class that you do not need an instance of but instead only need some data to use or call from.

Here is how static classes are written:

JavaScript:

```
var StaticTest = {
    x: function( xVal ) {
        return xVal;
    }
}
```

Ruby:

```
class StaticTest
    def self.x( xVal )
        return xVal
    end
end
```

C#:

```
public static class StaticTest
{
    public static int x( int xVal )
    {
        return xVal;
    }
}
```

These are very simple and all they do is return the value that was passed into them as the name *xVal*.

To call these:

JavaScript:

```
var y = StaticTest.x( 12 );
(y = 12)
```

Ruby:

```
y = StaticTest.x( 12 )
(y = 12)
```

continued...

C#:

```
int y = StaticTest.x( 12 );
(y = 12)
```

We will not be using static classes for our examples but it is important to know how to use them for when an opportunity arises to use them.

For loop

For loops are a way to loop through iterate through a min and maximum range, with a condition to perform a repetitive action. For loops in JavaScript and C# are written with the following rules:

```
for( initialValue; condition; increment )
```

In Ruby, they are written like:

```
for value in startValue..endValue
end
```

Ruby follows a few syntactical differences and generally, you won't be using for loops in the "traditional" way. Though still possible, Ruby handles looping a bit differently than some other languages. I will explain how to achieve the same result as the other languages, when using Ruby.

More clear example:

Javascript:
```
for( var i = 0; i < 100; i++ )
{
}
```

Ruby:
```
for i in 0..100
end
```

C#:
```
for( int i = 0; i < 100; i++ )
{
}
```

The for expression will continue to execute any code in this block as long as the condition is true. For each loop, the increment expression is called and the value is increased by whatever amount its set to; in this case, each loop will add 1 to *i*.

To break this down further:

i starts with the value of 0. As long as *i* is less than 100 the code in the for block is executed. After each execution of the for block, the value of *i* increments by 1.

This means this loop will execute 100 times as at the 101'st, the condition will no longer evaluate to true, as i is now equal to 100; no longer less than.

You can also create loops with more complex incrementation.

Javascript:
```
for( var i = 0; i < 100; i += 2 )
{
}
```

Ruby:
```
for i in 0..100
end
```

C#:
```
for( int i = 0; i < 100; i += 2 )
{
}
```

For JavaScript and C#, the loop will add 2 to *i* for every loop, meaning this loop will only run 50 times, as for each loop, 2 is added to *i* and it will reach 100 in 50 iterations. Ruby on the other hand doesn't have the same conditional statement as the other languages. To achieve the same result as JavaScript and C#, you could write the Ruby loop as such:

```
i = 0
while i < 100
    i += 2
end
```

We will touch on while loops in the next chapter and I will specifically show how to use them as a replacement to for loops, when using Ruby.

You could also have a different condition:

JavaScript:

```
for( var i = 0; i != 50; i += 2 )
{
}
```

Ruby:

```
i = 0
while i != 100
    i += 2
end
```

C#:

```
for( int i = 0; i != 50; i += 2 )
{
}
```

This loop will run 25 times, as *i* will hit the value of 50 in 25 iterations as 2 is added for each iteration. This is a bit more dangerous than using *i < 50* because let's say we had this incrementation instead:

JavaScript:

```
for( var i = 0; i != 50; i += 3 )
{
}
```

Ruby:

```
i = 0
while i != 100
    i += 3
end
```

C#:

```
for( int i = 0; i != 50; i += 3 )
{
}
```

This means *i* will never be equal to 50 and the loop will run forever, probably causing some sort of issue with your program; or simply freezing / crashing it. You have to be careful of the conditions you are using as if they never evaluate as false, the loop will run forever, continuing to run the code within them. Depending on the sort of code you are running in the for loop, it could cause a wide variety of problems.

Foreach

Many languages have adopted a sort of shorthand for handling for loops through an array of objects, called foreach loops. Foreach is not useful if you want to run a for loop like the examples above, where what you are looping through is something like an integer but if you want to loop through an array of objects, foreach is a great alternative to the for loop.

JavaScript:

```
for( var object in objects ) {
}
```

Ruby:

```
objects.each do |object|
end
```

C#:

```
foreach( ObjectType object in objects )
{
}
```

These will loop through each object as an object instead of you using *a* index to get the element. It doesn't do much of anything else different, it's simply a direct reference to the object in the object array instead of using an index get the element.

While loop

While loops are a lot like for loops in the sense that they will iterate continually until a condition is met. The major difference is that while loops will continue to loop until that condition is false and there is no incrementation during them.

While loops are written as such:;

JavaScript:
```
while( x > 0 )
{
}
```

Ruby:
```
while( x > 0 )
end
```

C#:
```
while( x > 0 )
{
}
```

x in these cases is just an example. To explain further:

JavaScript:
```
var x = 100;
while( x > 0 )
{
    x -= 1;
}
```

Ruby:
```
x = 100
while( x > 0 )
    x -= 1
end
```

C#:
```
int x = 100;
while( x > 0 )
{
    x -= 1;
}
```

In these while loops, *x* will start with 100 and then in the while loop, will be subtracted by 1, for each loop. When *x* is no longer greater than 0, the while loop will stop executing.

While loops are useful for managing bits of code that need to check a condition without an increment or starting value. Some examples of this are when your program needs to wait for something or when your program needs to loop for a longer period than what a for loop is normally used for.

The root of all programs hold a single while loop that continues to loop for the entire program. This is how the program knows to stay running until that condition is met; usually when the user decides to close the program.

An example of this:

JavaScript:

```
while( runProgram )
{
}
```

Ruby:

```
while( runProgram )
end
```

C#:

```
while( runProgram )
{
}
```

runProgram is a fictional bool value that as long as its true, will continue to loop. When this bool is set to false, the while loop will stop running and if the what is after the while loop is set to, close the program.

Basic problems

The next portion of the book will go over some more basic problems you might see when learning to program. These are designed to help you begin to break down programs into a program so the computer can then solve them for you.

> Reminder: **https://codepad.remoteinterview.io** is a fantastic website where you can follow along or work on these problems alone.

Ping Pong

The Ping Pong problem is common for early programmers as it's a simple problem that is easy to follow.

Overview:

Write a program that takes a whole number (integer) loops through each digit, from 1.

The program should output either the non divisible number as the number or if divisible, output the replacement; Ping, Pong, or PingPong.

Rules:

- Are numbers divisible by 3 are replaced with "Ping".
- Are numbers divisible by 5 are replaced with "Pong".
- Are numbers divisible by both 3 and 5 (or 15) are replaced with "PingPong".

> Remember, when I am explaining the code I will use *italics* to signify a portion of the code I am trying to explain.

> If you would like to try to solve this on your own, do so now. If you want to see the break down of the problem, go to the next page.

Ping Pong solution

Given the rules, we know that we have to access the digits between 1 and the value sent into the function. This sounds like a perfect job for a loop as it will allow us to loop as many times as the argument value. We will probably then want to store the result in an array so we can reference that array to get the divisible and non-divisible results from the loop.

To start, lets write the class and store the result in an array during a loop:

JavaScript:

```javascript
function PingPong( toValue ) {
    this.result = [];
    for( var index = 1; index < toValue + 1; index++ ) {

    }
}
```

Ruby:

```ruby
class PingPong
    attr_reader :result
    def initialize( toValue )
        @result = []
        for index in 1..toValue
        end
    end
end
```

C#:

```csharp
public class PingPong
{
    public PingPong( int toValue, out string[] result )
    {
        result = new String[toValue];
        for( int index = 1; index < toValue + 1; index++ )
        {
        }
    }
}
```

You'll notice that the loops in JavaScript and C# start with the value of 1. This is because we don't care about 0. In order to offset this, we need to add one to the high end of the loop as well, in our case *toValue*. Ruby for loops will always iterate to the max value, so we don't need to offset the value of *toValue*.

In the JavaScript class, we create a member variable by declaring it with *this.* first. This will allow us to access that variable after we have the object, which will hold the result from the for loop.

In the Ruby class, we are using something different: *attr_reader*. This is a way to declare a member variable within the class. In order to assign to this value in the class we reference it with the at(@) symbol, which we are declaring as the type of the array, using ([]).

In the C# class, we are using a string array because again, C# requires a type. This way we can store the values as a string in this array. Another thing to notice with C# is that we are using the out keyword in the *PingPong* constructor. This will allow us to create a string array and pass it into the new object as it is created and then get the result when it is done being created. Think of out as a way to send an existing reference into a function and have it changed instead of the function creating a copy of it. It is a sort of option compared to a function returning a value / object. Furthermore, unlike JavaScript and Ruby, C# requires us to have a size of the array. Because we know the size of the array should be the length of every digit between 1 and *toValue* + 1, we can think about the shift we did and instead keep this without the shift as keep 0 still counts as the first element of the array, so there will be the correct number of elements in the array to use for the result.

To explain the size of the C# string array further:

Let's say *toValue* was 5. We know that in our loop we don't care about 0 and need to add 1 to the *toValue* to offset that fact. But even when we do this, we know that the number of iterations in the for loop will still be 5, it just starts at 1 and ends at 5 instead of starting at 0 and ending at 4. This means that when we create the C# string array with the elements of the size of *toValue*, it will still be 5 elements: 0, 1, 2, 3, 4 resulting in the exact same space we need.
Filtering divisible from non-divisible:

Our next problem is how to filter the value of index into a divisible or non-divisible number. Because one of the rules is to check if the value of index is either 3 or 5, we should start with that first.

In order to check if a number is divisible by another, we can use the modulo operator and if the result of that division is 0 (meaning it is divisible as there is no remainder), we know that they are in fact divisible. Next, we can do either 3 or 5 as we have already checked the case of both of them being true.

From the Logical Operators section, you'll remember that we can connect these conditional statements with if / else if / elsif.

JavaScript:
```javascript
function PingPong( toValue ) {
    this.result = [];
    for( var index = 1; index < toValue + 1; index++ ) {
        if( index % 15 == 0 ) {

        } else if ( index % 5 == 0 ) {

        } else if( index % 3 == 0 ) {

        } else {

        }
    }
}
```

Ruby:
```ruby
class PingPong
    attr_reader :result
    def initialize( toValue )
        @result = []
        for index in 1..toValue
            if index % 15 == 0

            elsif index % 5 == 0

            elsif index % 3 == 0

            else

            end
        end
    end
end
```

continued...

C#:

```csharp
public class PingPong
{
    public PingPong( int toValue, out string[] result )
    {
        result = new String[toValue];
        for( int index = 1; index < toValue + 1; index++ )
        {
            if( index % 15 == 0 )
            {

            }
            else if ( index % 5 == 0 )
            {

            }
            else if( index % 3 == 0 )
            {

            }
            else
            {

            }
        }
    }
}
```

We don't use === for JavaScript because we know 15/5/3 are integers and we are comparing them with integers. Because we know this, we don't need to check the type though if you want to, you can change == to === in the conditional statements of JavaScript.

To reiterate, we start by checking if *index* is divisible by 15 first because if we checked 5 or 3 first, it would pass for either of them but not for both, if divisible. This would cause an issue of 15 never being checked because if its divisible by 3 and 5 that condition would pass and else if would never be called cause the condition was true.

We now have everything we need to in order to differentiate between what is divisible by 15/5/3 and what is not. The last thing we need to do is store the results in the result array.

JavaScript:

```javascript
function PingPong( toValue ) {
    this.result = [];
    for( var index = 1; index < toValue + 1; index++ ) {
        if( index % 15 == 0 ) {
            this.result.push( "PingPong" );
        } else if ( index % 5 == 0 ) {
            this.result.push( "Pong" );
        } else if( index % 3 == 0 ) {
            this.result.push( "Ping" );
        } else {
            this.result.push( index );
        }
    }
}

var testPing = new PingPong( 100 );
testPing.result.forEach( function(resultIndex ) {
    console.log( resultIndex );
});
```

Ruby:

```ruby
class PingPong
    attr_reader :result
    def initialize( toValue )
        @result = []
        for index in 1..toValue
            if index % 15 == 0
                @result.push( "PingPong" )
            elsif index % 5 == 0
                @result.push( "Pong" )
            elsif index % 3 == 0
                @result.push( "Ping" )
            else
                @result.push( index )
            end
        end
    end
end

testPing = PingPong.new( 100 )
testPing.result.each do |resultIndex|
    puts resultIndex
end
```

continued...

C#:

```csharp
public class PingPong
{
    public PingPong( int toValue, out string[] result )
    {
        result = new String[toValue];
        for( int index = 1; index < toValue + 1; index++ )
        {
            if( index % 15 == 0 )
            {
                result[index - 1] = "PingPong";
            }
            else if ( index % 5 == 0 )
            {
                result[index - 1] = "Pong";
            }
            else if( index % 3 == 0 )
            {
                result[index - 1] = "Ping";
            }
            else
            {
                result[index - 1] = index.ToString( );
            }
        }
    }
}

public class Test
{
    public static void Main()
    {
        string[] resultString = new String[0];
        PingPong test = new PingPong( 20, out resultString );

        foreach( string resultIndex in resultString )
        {
            Console.WriteLine( resultIndex );
        }
    }
}
```

As you can see, now that we know what index values are divisible, we can then add *PingPong*, Ping, or Pong in place of the index value. If none of the conditions pass, we simply add the index to the array as it is not divisible by 15/5/3. The outcome of this is that the result array will be populated with divisible and non-divisible values from 1 to the value of *toValue* + 1.

JavaScript and Ruby have what is called a dynamic array. This means that there is no defined size to the array and you can continually add or remove elements from it and it will adjust its size. With this feature, it comes with a function you can use to add an element to that array called *push*( ). This will add the object instance to the end of the array and adjust the size for you. C# does not.

In order to accomplish the same result with C#, we have to take into account the offset we did for index and what arrays do for storage. You will also remember from the variables section, arrays start with the index value of 0. This means that if we didn't offset the index back by one, we would start at index 1 and then go to 1 too many in the index range because we skipped 0. This would cause your C# compiler to complain and not compile the program.

Furthermore, because the C# array is not dynamic, we have to reference the index we want to assign the value to. We do this by using the [] brackets with the index value we want to reference. Because the index reference we want to assign to is that of the value of *index - 1*, we use that inside of the [] brackets ([index - 1]). This will ensure that the array stays within range and we fill it from 0 to the value of *toValue*.

Lastly, I want to bring up the importance of testing your code as you develop it. It is quite easy to forget something simple but if you run the code, it is often obvious as to what is wrong. As an example, a common mistake with this problem is to not test for 15 first, resulting in code that sometimes works. Whereas if you test the code, you'll notice right away that all instances of divisible by 15 will not be correct. Get used to compiling / running your code as you work. It will help you discover some results that are not desired.

That's it. This is an entry level problem because it dives into the basic concepts of data manipulation and how to handle conditions. There is a lot here to get used to, especially the differences in the three languages.

Prime, Even, Multiple of 10

This problem is again easy but will give you a different perspective on what it is to take in data and return a result.

Overview:

Create a function which checks a number for three different properties.

Rules:

- Is the number prime?
- Is the number even?
- Is the number a multiple of 10?
- Each should return true or false, which should be returned in an array.

> If you would like to try to solve this on your own, do so now. If you want to see the break down of the problem, go to the next page.

Prime, Even, Multiple of 10 solution

Given the rules, we know that the function must take in a single integer argument. With this argument, we then have to see if the number is prime, even, and/or a multiple of 10. The biggest task to solve this is to figure out how we can tell if a number is prime.

To start, let's figure out what makes a number prime.

A prime number can be divided evenly by only 1 and itself. The number must also be greater than 1.

With that in mind, we know that the number must be greater than 1. We can eliminate any number that is not greater than 1 as not prime from the start. We can also create the bool variables that will hold if the number is prime, even, or multiple of 10 as well as have a condition to make sure that the function argument is not 2. This is because of the way the loop will be written, 2 will be converted to false because 1 % 2 == 0 but in reality, 2 is a prime number. This is a sort of oddity when dealing with prime numbers but luckily, is the only case and it is easy to have a condition for before looping through each integer value.

JavaScript:
```
function MathTest( testInteger ) {
    var isPrime = true;
    var isEven = true;
    var isMultipleOf10 = true;

    if( testInteger <= 1 ) {
        isPrime = false;
    }
    else if( testInteger != 2 ) {

    }
}
```

Ruby:
```
class MathTest
    attr_reader :result
    def initialize( testInteger )
        isPrime = true
        isEven = true
        isMultipleOf10 = true;

        if testInteger <= 1
            isPrime = false
        elsif testInteger != 2
        end
    end
end
```

C#:

```
public class MathTest
{
    public MathTest( int testInteger, out bool[] result )
    {
        bool isPrime = true;
        bool isEven = true;
        bool isMultipleOf10 = true;

        if( testInteger <= 1 )
        {
            isPrime = false;
        }
        else if( testInteger != 2 )
        {

        }
    }
}
```

We start with the prime, even, and multiple of 10 bool variables set to true because we are eliminating them, not checking if they are any of these things; it is more straight forward to check if they don't meet these conditions than if they do.

Now that we have the bool variables and a condition to eliminate *isPrime* if it is less or equal than 1, we can now further check if it is not prime. This is done by using another loop. Because we want to check if *testInteger* is divisible by any other number, we have to loop through each integer between 2 and *testInteger - 1* (- 1 because the rules of a prime number is divisible by 1 and itself, so we don't need to loop to "itself").

JavaScript:

```javascript
function MathTest( testInteger ) {
    var isPrime = true;
    var isEven = true;
    var isMultipleOf10 = true;

    if( testInteger <= 1 ) {
        isPrime = false;
    }
    else if( testInteger != 2 ) {
        for( var each = 0; each <= testInteger - 1; each++ ) {
            if( testInteger % each == 0 ) {
                isPrime = false;
                break;
            }
        }
    }
}
```

Ruby:

```ruby
class MathTest
    attr_reader :result
    def initialize( testInteger )
        isPrime = true
        isEven = true
        isMultipleOf10 = true;

        if testInteger <= 1
            isPrime = false
        elsif testInteger != 2
            for each in 2..testInteger - 1
                if testInteger % each == 0
                    isPrime = false
                end
            end
        end
    end
end
```

continued...

C#:

```csharp
public class MathTest
{
    public MathTest( int testInteger, out bool[] result )
    {
        bool isPrime = true;
        bool isEven = true;
        bool isMultipleOf10 = true;

        if( testInteger < 1 )
        {
            isPrime = false;
        }
        else if( testInteger != 2 )
        {
            for(int each = 2; each <= testInteger - 1; each++)
            {
                if( testInteger % each == 0 )
                {
                    isPrime = false;
                    break;
                }
            }
        }
    }
}
```

Our for loop starts with the value of 2. This is again because of the rules, it has to be greater than 1 and we already have a condition for 2. The condition for the loop is to check if each is less than or equal to *testInteger - 1*, as we don't need to loop to the value of *testInteger* as all numbers will be divisible by itself.

In the loop block, we check to see if the remainder of *testInteger* divided by each is 0. If this is the case, we know that *testInteger* is divisible by something other than 1 and itself, meaning its not prime. If that is the case, we set *isPrime* to false and use a keyword called break to exit out of the loop. Technically you do not need break but it will have a very small performance increase as the loop wont continue and check for anymore remainders between *testInteger* and each.

Because *isPrime* starts as true and if *testInteger* is prime, the for loop will never change it to false, so that is all we have to do to see if a number is prime.

The next task is to check if *testInteger* is even. If the remainder of *testInteger % 2 != 0* is 0, then it is even.

JavaScript:

```javascript
function MathTest( testInteger ) {
    var isPrime = true;
    var isEven = true;
    var isMultipleOf10 = true;

    if( testInteger <= 1 ) {
        isPrime = false;
    }
    else if( testInteger != 2 ) {
        for( var each = 0; each <= testInteger - 1; each++ ) {
            if( testInteger % each == 0 ) {
                isPrime = false;
                break;
            }
        }
    }

    if( testInteger % 2 != 0 ) {
        isEven = false;
    }
}
```

Ruby:

```ruby
class MathTest
    attr_reader :result
    def initialize( testInteger )
        isPrime = true
        isEven = true
        isMultipleOf10 = true;

        if testInteger <= 1
            isPrime = false
        elsif testInteger != 2
            for each in 2..testInteger - 1
                if testInteger % each == 0
                    isPrime = false
                end
            end
        end

        if testInteger % 2 != 0
            isEven = false
        end
    end
end
```

continued...

C#:

```csharp
public class MathTest
{
    public MathTest( int testInteger, out bool[] result )
    {
        bool isPrime = true;
        bool isEven = true;
        bool isMultipleOf10 = true;

        if( testInteger < 1 )
        {
            isPrime = false;
        }
        else if( testInteger != 2 )
        {
            for(int each = 2; each <= testInteger - 1; each++)
            {
                if( testInteger % each == 0 )
                {
                    isPrime = false;
                    break;
                }
            }
        }

        if( testInteger % 2 != 0 )
        {
            isEven = false;
        }
    }
}
```

There isn't much more to say here. That is all that it takes to see if a number is even (or odd).

The last part is to check if *testInteger* is a multiple of 10. You may have already guessed it, it is done in the exact same way as seeing if the number is even. *testInteger % 10 == 0* (is multiple of 10).

We can also finish up the function and return/out the results array with the three bool varaibles: *isPrime*, *isEven*, and *isMultipleOf10*.

JavaScript:

```
function MathTest( testInteger ) {
    var isPrime = true;
    var isEven = true;
    var isMultipleOf10 = true;

    if( testInteger <= 1 ) {
        isPrime = false;
    }
    else if( testInteger != 2 ) {
        for( var each = 0; each <= testInteger - 1; each++ ) {
            if( testInteger % each == 0 ) {
                isPrime = false;
                break;
            }
        }
    }

    if( testInteger % 2 != 0 ) {
        isEven = false;
    }

    if( testInteger % 10 != 0 ) {
        isMultipleOf10 = false;
    }

    return [ isPrime, isEven, isMultipleOf10 ];
}

var test = new MathTest( 100 );

test.forEach( function( r ) {
    console.log( r );
});
```

continued...

Ruby:

```ruby
class MathTest
    attr_reader :result
    def initialize( testInteger )
        isPrime = true
        isEven = true
        isMultipleOf10 = true;

        if testInteger <= 1
            isPrime = false
        elsif testInteger != 2
            for each in 2..testInteger - 1
                if testInteger % each == 0
                    isPrime = false
                    break
                end
            end
        end

        if testInteger % 2 != 0
            isEven = false
        end

        if testInteger % 10 != 0
            isMultipleOf10 = false
        end

        @result = [ isPrime, isEven, isMultipleOf10 ]
    end
end

test.result.each do |r|
    puts r
end
```

C#:

```csharp
public class MathTest
{
    public MathTest( int testInteger, out bool[] result )
    {
        bool isPrime = true;
        bool isEven = true;
        bool isMultipleOf10 = true;

        if( testInteger < 1 )
        {
            isPrime = false;
        }
        else if( testInteger != 2 )
        {
            for(int each = 2; each <= testInteger - 1; each++)
            {
                if( testInteger % each == 0 )
                {
                    isPrime = false;
                    break;
                }
            }
        }
        if( testInteger % 2 != 0 )
        {
            isEven = false;
        }
        if( testInteger % 10 != 0 )
        {
            isMultipleOf10 = false;
        }

        result = new bool[3];
        result[0] = isPrime;
        result[1] = isEven;
        result[2] = isMultipleOf10;
    }
}

public class Test
{
    public static void Main()
    {
        bool[] result = new bool[0];
        MathTest test = new MathTest( 100, out result );

        foreach( bool r in result )
        {
            Console.WriteLine( r );
        }
    }
}
```

The main purpose of this test is to further explore the use of the modulo operator (%) and see the power it gives you when wanting to search for specific types of numbers. It also gives you more practice when creating and using arrays to store a chunk of data.

Is Palindrome

A palindrome is a sequence of characters that read the same forward or backwards.

Here are a few common examples:
- Racecar
- Reviver
- Kayak
- Level
- Noon

They can also be sentences:
- Rise to vote sir
- Was it a cat I saw

Or just gibberish:
- Adkfjowojfkda
- Owjrlenelrjwo

Overview:

Create a function that takes in a string and returns if it is a palindrome or not; true or false.

Rules:
- Does the string read the same forwards and backwards?
- Does the function true if it does?
- Does the function false if it does not?

If you would like to try to solve this on your own, do so now. If you want to see the break down of the problem, go to the next page.

Is Palindrome solution

Given the rules, we know that a palindrome is a string that reads the same forwards and backwards. With this in mind, the answer to the solution is quite simple: reverse the string and see if it matches the first. This means we have to create a copy of the function argument, reverse it, then compare it with the original. Return true if they are the same, false if not.

JavaScript:

```javascript
function isPalindrome( phrase ) {
    var reversed = "";
    for( var character = phrase.length - 1; character >= 0;
character-- ) {
        reversed += phrase[character];
    }
    this.palindrome = ( reversed == phrase );
}
```

Ruby:

```ruby
class IsPalindrome
    attr_reader :isPalindrome
    def initialize( phrase )
        reversed = ""
        character = phrase.length - 1
        while character >= 0
            reversed += phrase[character]
            character -= 1
        end
        @isPalindrome = ( phrase == reversed )
    end
end
```

C#:

```csharp
public class IsPalindrome
{
    public IsPalindrome( string phrase, out bool isPalindrome )
    {
        string reversed = "";
        for( int character = phrase.Length - 1; character >= 0;
character-- )
        {
            reversed += phrase[character];
        }

        isPalindrome = ( reversed == phrase );
    }
}
```

One thing that stands out here is that we are using for loops differently; or while loop for ruby. In the case of wanting to reverse a string, we need to loop through the string backwards and then store each character into another string, in our case reversed. This means reversed will be populated for each loop with the individual character from the phrase, in reverse. To loop through the string in reverse, we start with the max size of the phrase, with *phrase.length* and then count down to 0.

So far, this will solve for a phrase that doesn't have any kind of capital letters. As an example, right now, "racecar" will return true; it is a palindrome. However, "Racecar" will not. This is because when we compare the two strings, it factors in case as well. In order to solve this, we need to convert the phrase to either all lower case letters or all upper case letters. Lower case is what I will be doing.

JavaScript:
```javascript
function isPalindrome( phrase ) {
    var reversed = "";
    var phraseLower = reversed.toLowerCase( );
    for( var character = phraseLower.length - 1; character >= 0;
character-- ) {
        reversed += phraseLower[character];
    }
    this.palindrome = ( reversed == phraseLower );
}

console.log( new isPalindrome( "RacECar sis
racEcar" ).palindrome );
```
Ruby:
```ruby
class IsPalindrome
    attr_reader :isPalindrome
    def initialize( phrase )
        reversed = ""
        phraseLower = phrase.downcase
        character = phraseLower.length - 1
        while character >= 0
            reversed += phraseLower[character]
            character -= 1
        end
        @isPalindrome = ( phraseLower == reversed )
    end
end

puts IsPalindrome.new( "RacECar sis racEcar" ).isPalindrome
```

C#:

```csharp
public class IsPalindrome
{
    public IsPalindrome( string phrase, out bool isPalindrome )
    {
        string reversed = "";
        string phraseLower = phrase.ToLower( );
        for( int character = phraseLower.Length - 1; character >=
0; character-- )
        {
            reversed += phraseLower[character];
        }

        isPalindrome = ( reversed == phraseLower );
    }
}

public class Test
{
    public static void Main()
    {
        bool isPalindrome;
        IsPalindrome testPalindrome = new IsPalindrome( "RacEcar
sis racEcar", out isPalindrome );
        Console.WriteLine( isPalindrome );
    }
}
```

This problem is on the easier side but supports the utility of for loops, as in the conditions and the way the iteration works can be what you want; meaning you can increment or decrement the value through the loop. This problem also helps you identify the uniqueness of dealing with strings and how to manipulate them.

Scrabble Score

Overview:

Write a method that takes a word and returns the Scrabble score for that word. Here are the values of letters in Scrabble:

A, E, I, O, U, L, N, R, S, T	1
D, G	2
B, C, M, P	3
F, H, V, W, Y	4
K	5
J, X	8
Q, Z	10

Rules:
- Does the function argument contain more than one word? If so, return "You can only check one word or letter."
- Does the function argument contain a number? If so, return "Your word containers a number. This is not allowed."
- Is the function argument within the above guidelines? If so, return the score of the word as an integer value.

> If you would like to try to solve this on your own, do so now. If you want to see the break down of the problem, go to the next page.

Scrabble Score solution

If you don't know, Scrabble is a board game where you take your random letters and try to make words from the existing letters / words on the board. Some letters are worth more than others, as some letters are more rare than others.

In order for us to effectively calculate the scores, we must first know the score of each letter. In the overview for this problem is the breakdown for how much each letter is worth, in points. Let's start by writing our classes with that data stored in them.

JavaScript:

```javascript
function ScrabbleScore( word ) {
    var scores = { "aeioulnrst": 1,
                   "dg"        : 2,
                   "bcmp"      : 3,
                   "fhvwy"     : 4,
                   "k"         : 5,
                   "jx"        : 8,
                   "qz"        : 10 };
}
```

Ruby:

```ruby
class ScrabbleScore
    def initialize( word )
        scores = { "aeioulnrst"=> 1,
                   "dg"        => 2,
                   "bcmp"      => 3,
                   "fhvwy"     => 4,
                   "k"         => 5,
                   "jx"        => 8,
                   "qz"        => 10 }
    end
end
```

continued...

C#:

```
using System.Collections;

public class ScrabbleScore
{
    public ScrabbleScore( string word, out int wordScore )
    {
        Hashtable scores = new Hashtable( );
        scores.Add("aeioulnrst",  1);
        scores.Add("dg"         ,  2);
        scores.Add("bcmp"       ,  3);
        scores.Add("fhvwy"      ,  4);
        scores.Add("k"          ,  5);
        scores.Add("jx"         ,  8);
        scores.Add("qz"         , 10);

        wordScore = 0;
    }
}
```

> If using C#, make sure to include using **System.Collections** under using System. Hash tables won't work unless you do.

The scores are being stored in what's called a hash table. This is like an array but instead of being referenced by index, elements are referenced by a key and for each key, there is a value. For our purposes, we are storing all the letters together that are worth that value; so *aeioulnrst* are worth 1 point and *dg* are worth 2. This will allow us to find the letters worth by referencing the value in the key of the hash elements.

To get the score for each letter, we have to first loop through each letter of the word and then loop through the hash tables elements to see if that character of word exists in the hash element. If it does, we can get the score from the hash. If it doesn't we need to loop through the next hash element to see if the character is in that.

JavaScript:

```
function ScrabbleScore( word ) {
    var scores = { "aeioulnrst": 1,
                   "dg"        : 2,
                   "bcmp"      : 3,
                   "fhvwy"     : 4,
                   "k"         : 5,
                   "jx"        : 8,
                   "qz"        : 10 };
    this.wordScore = 0;
    word = word.toLowerCase( );
    for( var character = 0; character < word.length; character++ )
{

        for(var score in scores) {
            if( score.indexOf( word[character] ) > -1 ) {
                this.wordScore += scores[score];
            }
        }
    }
}

console.log( new ScrabbleScore( "Apple" ).wordScore );
```

Ruby:

```
class ScrabbleScore
    attr_reader :wordScore
    def initialize( word )
        scores = { "aeioulnrst"=> 1,
                   "dg"        => 2,
                   "bcmp"      => 3,
                   "fhvwy"     => 4,
                   "k"         => 5,
                   "jx"        => 8,
                   "qz"        => 10 }
        @wordScore = 0
        splitWord = word.split(//)
        splitWord.each do |character|
            scores.keys.each do |score|
                splitScore = score.split(//)
                if splitScore.include? character.downcase
                    @wordScore += scores.fetch( score )
                end
            end
        end
    end
end

puts ScrabbleScore.new( "Apple" ).wordScore
```

continued...

C#:

```csharp
using System.Collections;

public class ScrabbleScore
{
    public ScrabbleScore( string word, out int wordScore )
    {
        Hashtable scores = new Hashtable( );
        scores.Add("aeioulnrst", 1);
        scores.Add("dg"        , 2);
        scores.Add("bcmp"      , 3);
        scores.Add("fhvwy"     , 4);
        scores.Add("k"         , 5);
        scores.Add("jx"        , 8);
        scores.Add("qz"        , 10);

        wordScore = 0;
        word = word.ToLower( );
        for( int character = 0; character < word.Length; character++ )
        {
            foreach (DictionaryEntry score in scores)
            {
                if( score.Key.ToString( ).IndexOf( word[character] ) > -1 )
                {
                    wordScore += (int)score.Value;
                }
            }
        }
    }
}

public class Test
{
    public static void Main()
    {
        int wordScore = 0;
        new ScrabbleScore( "Apple", out wordScore );
        Console.WriteLine( wordScore );
    }
}
```

Like with the palindrome solution, we have to convert the string into all lower case. This is because again, characters in strings are different if capitalized. We are also starting *wordScore* with the value of 0 so that it both has the type of integer but also so we can add to it and conclude the final value of *wordScore* is the correct score.

Each of these languages handle hash tables a bit differently from each other, so I am going to break down each.

Because hash tables have a key and value pair for each element, we have to access each differently. To access the key, we can use the var score in scores, in the for loop. What this is saying is, score is going to be the reference name for each of the elements in scores. This way, when we use score, we know that it'll be one of the scores. In the condition, we use a utility function called *indexOf* which takes in an argument of a character from word, accessed by using the array notation of passing in the character index as the character of the word: word[character]. If the return value of *indexOf* is greater than -1, we know that the score(from scores) includes the character from word. With that condition true, we can then add to the *wordScore* with the value of score, accessed again by using the array notation scores[score]. This works because score is like the index from a normal for loop, but instead of an integer value, it is the whole key; such as "*aeioulnrst*" would be the index of the first *scores* element and give us the value that we set(the score of the letter).

Ruby has us again use *attr_reader* to store the *wordScore*, which we also set to 0 at the start. Ruby also handles strings a bit differently so we use the split function to convert the string into an array and by using the // as the argument for split, it creates an array storing every character in the string as an element in the array. With the string converted into an array, we can then use the *.each do |element|* loop to access each character of the string. The keys for scores is also a string, so again, we convert that into an array to loop through each character of the string. In the condition we use a utility function called *include?*. This is a function that Ruby gives us to see if the array (in our case the array of characters from the *splitScore* string), includes the current element of *splitWord*, known as character. If this condition is true, we know the character exists in the score and we add to the *wordScore* by using another hash utility function called fetch( ). This will look into the hash and match the key of score and return the value of that key; in our case, the score.

C# again uses the out argument keyword for wordScore so it will give us the score back, with it initially set at 0. We also convert the word argument to all lowercase using the ToLower( ) utility function, like what we used for the palindrome test. Then, we loop through the word and for every element of the word, we loop through the hash table using the foreach loop. Score in this case is the type of DictionaryEntry, which is C#'s name for an element in a hash table. The condition has a few things going on. The first is that we convert the score.Key to a string, using the ToString( ) function. We then call IndexOf from the converted key as a string to see if the current character of the word (word[character]) is included in the key, which we know it does if the return value of IndexOf is greater than -1; meaning it found a character that matches the word element as character. Once that is true, we then add to wordScore with the score.Value. You'll notice that there is something we haven't done before with what's being added to wordScore. (int)score.Value is what is call a cast. Because score.Value is actually an object, we have to convert it into an integer so we can add it to wordScore. It is important to keep in mind that casting is not a universal thing. The types you are casting need to be of the same inheritance (or the language needs to support the conversion). As an example, you can't convert a complex object with an integer, though you could take a single string value in the complex object and convert it into an integer, if the string is a number. Casting is a somewhat complicated thing and I recommend that you look into how C# handles casting between types, as they do have some unique ways of doing so.

Letter Count

Overview:

To further practice how to search through strings and understand what is in them, the letter count problem is designed around the concept of storing the number of times each letter in a string is used and return a hash table of the letters as keys, with the value being how many times its used.

Rules:
- Does your function return a hash table that includes how many times each letter was used in that string?
- Does the hash table ignore spaces?

If you would like to try to solve this on your own, do so now. If you want to see the break down of the problem, go to the next page.

Letter Count solution

This problem is a bit of an extension from the Scrabble Score problem and the only complication is the process of storing when to store a new letter key into a hash table or when to update an existing letter key with a new value.

JavaScript:

```
function LetterCount( word ) {
    this.countHash = { };
    for( var character = 0; character < word.length; character++ )
{

    }
}
```

Ruby:

```
class LetterCount
    attr_reader :countHash
    def intialize( word )
        @countHash = { }
        splitWord = word.split(//)
        splitWord.each do |character|

        end
    end
end
```

C#:

```
using System.Collections;

public class LetterSort
{
    public LetterSort( string word, out Hashtable countHash )
    {
        countHash = new Hashtable( );
        for( int character = 0; character < word.Length; character+
+ )
        {

        }
    }
}
```

> If using **C#**, remember to add using **System.Collections;**
> under **using System;**

This should look a bit familiar to you, as all we are doing is looping through the word that is being passed into the object when it is created. The next step is to start to see if the characters of the word exist in the hash table, if they do add to the value of that character key. If they don't exist, add a new hash to the table with the key as the character of the word and the value set to 1, as it's only been used once when creating it.

JavaScript:

```javascript
function LetterCount( word ) {
    this.countHash = { };
    for( var character = 0; character < word.length; character++ )
    {
        if( this.countHash[word[character]] === undefined ) {
            this.countHash[word[character]] = 1;
        } else {
            this.countHash[word[character]] += 1;
        }
    }
}
```

Ruby:

```ruby
class LetterCount
    attr_reader :countHash
    def initialize( word )
        @countHash = { }
        splitWord = word.split(//)
        splitWord.each do |character|
            if !@countHash.key? character
                @countHash[character] = 1
            else
                @countHash[character] += 1
            end
        end
    end
end
```

continued...

C#:

```csharp
using System.Collections;

public class LetterSort
{
    public LetterSort( string word, out Hashtable countHash )
    {
        countHash = new Hashtable( );
        for( int character = 0; character < word.Length; character+
+ )
        {
            if( !countHash.ContainsKey( word[character] ) )
            {
                countHash.Add( word[character], 1 );
            }
            else
            {
                countHash[ word[character] ] =
(int)countHash[ word[character] ] + 1;
            }
        }
    }
}
```

We have a for loop that iterates though every character in the word. If that word is not in the hash table, we add the hash with a key and value pair; the value being 1. If that condition fails, as in there is an existing hash with that key in the table, we get a reference to the hash element using the key and add 1 to it.

In JavaScript, our condition checks if the hash table is undefined. This is because JavaScript will allow you to access an element of the hash table if it doesn't exist without much of an issue. It will simply say that what is there is undefined. Because of this, we can say that if the element of a hash table is undefined, it hasn't been created yet. To assign or reference an element in the hash table, we use the character of the word as the key, accessed with the array notation (*[word[character]]*) and assign 1 to it if it hasn't been assigned, or if it exists already, add 1 to the value.

In Ruby, we have a helper function called *key?* Which is going to look into the hash table for you and return true if it does already exist or false, if it doesn't exist. Like JavaScript, if it doesn't exist, we create the reference in the hash table using the character as the key or add to the value of the hash reference by accessing the element and adding 1 to it.

In C#, we have a utility function called *ContainsKey* will like Ruby, will return true if a hash does exist and false if it doesn't. If it doesn't we use the *Hashtable* class functioned called Add to add a key as the *word[character]* with the starting value of 1. If it already exists, we have to get a reference to that hash using the *word[character]* as the key and then say the value of that is equal to the cast version of the current value plus 1.

If you were to test this, you'll notice that the hash table is going to accept spaces as a character, which goes against the rules of the problem. Let's add a condition to make sure the current element isn't a space before creating/adding to the hash table.

JavaScript:

```
function LetterCount( word ) {
    this.countHash = { };
    for( var character = 0; character < word.length; character++ )
{
        if( word[character] !== ' ' ) {
            if( this.countHash[word[character]] === undefined ) {
                this.countHash[word[character]] = 1;
            } else {
                this.countHash[word[character]] += 1;
            }
        }
    }
}

console.log( new LetterCount( "testing spaces" ).countHash );
```

Ruby:

```
class LetterCount
    attr_reader :countHash
    def initialize( word )
        @countHash = { }
        splitWord = word.split(//)
        splitWord.each do |character|
            if character != " "
                if !@countHash.key? character
                    @countHash[character] = 1
                else
                    @countHash[character] += 1
                end
            end
        end
    end
end
puts LetterCount.new( "testing spaces" ).countHash
```

continued...

C#:

```csharp
using System;
using System.Collections;

public class LetterSort
{
    public LetterSort( string word, out Hashtable countHash )
    {
        countHash = new Hashtable( );
        for( int character = 0; character < word.Length; character+
+ )
        {
            if( word[character] != ' ' )
            {
                if( !countHash.ContainsKey( word[character] ) )
                {
                    countHash.Add( word[character], 1 );
                }
                else
                {
                    countHash[ word[character] ] =
(int)countHash[ word[character] ] + 1;
                }
            }
        }
    }
}

public class Test
{
    public static void Main()
    {
        Hashtable countHash = new Hashtable( );
        LetterSort sort = new LetterSort( "testing spaces", out
countHash );
        foreach( DictionaryEntry count in countHash )
        {
            Console.Write( count.Key );
            Console.WriteLine( ": " + count.Value.ToString( ) );
        }
    }
}
```

The added condition is simply a check if the current element of the word is a space (' ') or
(" "), depending on the language.

Checking to see if the current character is basic. It's mainly a syntax change between languages as to what the type of the character represents. Generally, double quotes around a string (*"hello"*) is a string whereas a single quote around a letter is a character (*'a'*). This is apparent in JavaScript and C# but Ruby has a different rule set and you can technically use either and the language will understand.

This problem is made a bit more difficult to solve as it factors in the technical use of how these languages use hash tables. The logic itself isn't nearly as complicated as figuring out how to work with the language tools.

Intermediate problems

The next portion of the book will go over an intermediate problem that you might see when you are moving into a career as a programmer.

These problems are going to be just a notch above the others in difficulty. They aren't a big leap from what you've learned so far.

Bubble sort

Sorting algorithms are a big part of performance when dealing with larger projects as trying to find something in an array that is sorted is often much easier than trying to find that same element in the array if it wasn't sorted. This is because when using loops on an unsorted array, you have to look at each element at a time to see if it that element is the one you're looking for. Bubble sort is the first rudimentary step to sorting algorithms and ideally isn't used for big arrays as compared to other sorting algorithms, it is not as efficient. With that said, it is still a precursor to understanding the more complicated algorithms.

You will find that all languages offer you a utility function to sort or at least a library that does it for you but it is still a good thing to understand a little of the logic.

Overview:

Bubble sorting is a simple sorting algorithm that repeatedly steps through an array, comparing each with the last and then swaps them if the current element of the array is in the wrong order.

Rules:
- Create a function that sorts an array.
- Create a object that has a random integer value.
- Create an array of these objects.
- Create a function that takes in a array of objects and sorts them by an integer value within the object, returning a new array of sorted objects.

> If you would like to try to solve this on your own, do so now. If you want to see the break down of the problem, go to the next page.

Bubble Sort solution

The main idea of a bubble sort is to use a while loop to continually loop through the elements in an array and see if the current element of an array has an attribute that is more than the next in the array. If it is, you swap the two, moving the lower attribute down in the array and the higher attribute up in the array.

To break down an individual example of this:

```
Apples[index].weight > apples[index + 1].weight
toSwap = apples[index]
apples[index] = apples[index + 1]
apples[index + 1] = toSwap
```

As you can see, we have to store the apple we want to swap, then swap the current apple in the array with the next one, then we assign the next apple in the array with the one to swap, which is the current one. As the while loop continues to run, it continues to do this.

For this example I am going to use a class called Apple and it will have a variable called *weight*. I will use weight to sort the apples.

JavaScript:

```
function Apple( appleWeight ) {
    this.weight = appleWeight;
}

function apple_sort( apples ) {
    var swapping = true;
    while( swapping ) {

    }
    return apples;
}

var apples = [];
for( var i = 0; i < 100; i++ ) {
    var apple = new Apple( Math.floor( ( Math.random( ) * 200) +
1 ) );
    apples.push( apple );
    console.log( apple.weight )
}
```

Ruby:

```ruby
class Apple
    attr_reader :weight
    def initialize( appleWeight )
        @weight = appleWeight
    end
end

def apple_sort( apples )
    swapping = true
    while swapping

    end
    return apples
end

apples = []
for i in 1..100
    apple = Apple.new( rand( 1..200 ) )
    apples.push( apple )
    puts apple.weight
end
```

C#:

```csharp
public class Apple
{
    public int weight;
    public Apple( int appleWeight )
    {
        this.weight = appleWeight;
    }
}

public class Test
{
    public static Apple[] apple_sort( Apple[] apples )
    {
        bool swapping = true;
        while( swapping )
        {
            swapping = false;
        }
        return apples;
    }

    public static void Main()
    {
        Apple[] apples = new Apple[100];
        Random randomNumber = new Random( );
        for( int i = 0; i < apples.Length; i++ )
        {
            Apple newApple = new
Apple( randomNumber.Next( 0,200 ) );
            apples[ i ] = ( newApple );
            Console.WriteLine( newApple.weight );
        }
    }
}
```

As you can see, we have the main class we want to sort called Apple. Apple has a weight that we can use as the value to sort by. We then create 100 apples with a random weight value between 1 and 200; which is a purely academic value. We also have a function called apple_sort that will be used to sort the apples. In that function we setup the initial while loop with its condition and a return value to return the array of sorted apples.

If you run the code now, you can see that we are creating 100 apples all with a random *weight*, which is being printed out with *console.log()* (JavaScript), *puts* (Ruby), or *Console. WriteLine(C#)*.

With this in place, we can now sort the apples by adding the swap logic to the apple_sort function:

JavaScript:

```
function Apple( appleWeight ) {
    this.weight = appleWeight;
}

function apple_sort( apples ) {
    var swapping = true;
    while( swapping ) {
        swapping = false;
        for( var index = 0; index < apples.length - 1; index++ ) {
            if( apples[ index ].weight > apples[ index + 1 ].weight
) {
                var swapApple = apples[ index ];
                apples[ index ] = apples[ index + 1 ];
                apples[ index + 1 ] = swapApple;
                swapping = true;
            }
        }
    }
    return apples;
}

var apples = [];
for( var i = 0; i < 100; i++ ) {
    apples.push( new Apple( Math.floor( ( Math.random( ) * 200) + 1
) ) );
}

apples = apple_sort( apples );
for( var i = 0; i < apples.length; i++ ) {
    console.log( apples[ i ].weight );
}
```

Ruby:

```ruby
class Apple
    attr_reader :weight
    def initialize( appleWeight )
        @weight = appleWeight
    end
end

def apple_sort( apples )
    swapping = true
    while swapping
        swapping = false
        ( apples.length - 1 ).times do |index|
            if apples[ index ].weight > apples[ index + 1 ].weight
                lightApple = apples[ index ]
                apples[ index ] = apples[ index + 1 ]
                apples[ index + 1 ] = lightApple
                swapping = true
            end
        end
    end
    return apples
end

apples = []
for i in 1..100
    apple = Apple.new( rand( 1..200 ) )
    apples.push( apple )
end

apples = apple_sort( apples )
apples.each do |apple|
    puts apple.weight
end
```

continued...

C#:

```csharp
public class Apple
{
    public int weight;
    public Apple( int appleWeight )
    {
        this.weight = appleWeight;
    }
}

public class Test
{
    public static Apple[] apple_sort( Apple[] apples )
    {
        bool swapping = true;
        while( swapping )
        {
            swapping = false;
            for( int index = 0; index < apples.Length - 1; index++ )
            {
                if( apples[ index ].weight > apples[ index + 1 ].weight )
                {
                    Apple swapApple = apples[ index ];
                    apples[ index ] = apples[ index + 1 ];
                    apples[ index + 1 ] = swapApple;
                    swapping = true;
                }
            }
        }
        return apples;
    }

    public static void Main()
    {
        Apple[] apples = new Apple[100];
        Random randomNumber = new Random( );
        for( var i = 0; i < apples.Length; i++ )
        {
            apples[ I ] = ( new Apple( randomNumber.Next( 0,200 ) ) );
        }

        apples = apple_sort( apples );
        for( int i = 0; i < apples.Length; i++ )
        {
            Console.WriteLine( apples[ i ].weight );
        }
    }
}
```

That is a bubble sort example using a custom class with an attribute to sort by. To break this down a bit more, the while loop will continue to run as long as the condition of the current apples weight is more than the next apples. As soon as there is no set of apples that meets this condition, the while loop will exist because swapping will still be false from the beginning of the loop and then the function will return the sorted apples array.

There are many sorting algorithms that are much more efficient than this one but again, this is a good start to understand the basic logic on how to sort objects, especially if there aren't many to sort.

Digitize and Sort

This problem will utilize what you have learned so far and have you solve in combination.

Overview:

Given a non-negative integer, return an array of the individual digits in sorted order. An example:

If the function argument is 8675309, the return array will be: [0,3,5,6,7,8,9].

Rules:
- Does your function take in an integer value and return an array?
- Does your function sort the array into least to most before returning?

> If you would like to try to solve this on your own, do so now. If you want to see the break down of the problem, go to the next page.

Digitize and Sort solution

This problem is the first where we have to think of it has two individual problems that work together for one result. The first is converting a whole number into an array of those individual numbers and the next is how to sort those numbers in an array.

To start, let's figure out how to get the whole number into an array of all the individual numbers:

JavaScript:
```javascript
function Digitize(number) {
    var asString = number.toString();
    var asArray = [];
    for(var index = 0; index < asString.length; index++) {
        asArray.push(parseInt(asString[index]));
    }
}
```

Ruby:
```ruby
def digitize( number )
    asString = number.to_s
    asArray = asString.split(//)
end
```

C#:
```csharp
public static int[] Digitize(int number)
{
    string asString = number.ToString( );
    int[] asArray = new int[asString.Length];
    for(int idx = 0; idx < asString.Length; idx++)
    {
        asArray[idx] = Convert.ToInt32(asString[idx].ToString());
    }
}
```

The process of converting a whole number into a string is fairly straight forward and the reason we do this is that the conversion of a string into an array, or the ability to loop through that string to create an array, is also easy. The one thing to keep in mind here is to use the tools given to you by these languages in ways that might not seem so straight forward, especially when you want to convert types from one to another.

C# and JavaScript conversion from string to integer is done through a helper method (*parseInt* for JavaScript and *Convert.ToInt32 for* C#). These are utility functions that will convert a string to an integer, if the string has a result as an integer. C# varies here a bit because we are converting a*sString[idx]* to a string, using the *ToString( )* function. The reason for this is that the *Convert.ToInt32* function is looking for a string type but we are passing it a character. If you were to run this without the secondary cast to a string, from the character, the result from *ToInt32* would not be correct. This is because a character and a string are technically different types but in programming languages, can be looked at in the same way, so the *ToInt32* function wont fail but it also wont cast the character as correctly as it would a string.

Ruby's *split* function is designed to convert a string and put it into an array, so we don't need a for loop to create it ourselves. As long as you pass in the double back slash (*//*) as the argument for *Split*, the result will be an array of every character in the string as an array, which in our case will the individual numbers of the number argument.

The next step is to take the array we have created from the argument called number and sort it, then return the sorted result:

JavaScript:

```javascript
function Digitize(number) {
  var asString = number.toString();
  var asArray = [];
  for(var index = 0; index < asString.length; index++){
      asArray.push(parseInt(asString[index]));
  }

  var swapping = true;
  while(swapping) {
      swapping = false;
      for(var nIdx = 0; nIdx < asArray.length - 1; nIdx++){
          if( asArray[nIdx] > asArray[nIdx + 1]){
              var swapNumber = asArray[nIdx];
              asArray[nIdx] = asArray[nIdx + 1];
              asArray[nIdx + 1] = swapNumber;
              swapping = true;
          }
      }
  }
  return asArray;
}

console.log( Digitize( 987654321 ) );
```

Ruby:

```ruby
def digitize( number )
    asString = number.to_s
    asArray = asString.split(//)

    swapping = true
    while swapping
        swapping = false
        ( asArray.length - 1 ).times do |nIdx|
            if asArray[ nIdx ] > asArray[nIdx + 1]
                swapNumber = asArray[nIdx]
                asArray[nIdx] = asArray[nIdx + 1]
                asArray[nIdx + 1] = swapNumber
                swapping = true
            end
        end
    end
    return asArray
end

puts digitize( 987654321 )
```

continued...

C#:

```csharp
public class Test
{
    public static int[] Digitize( int number )
    {
        string asString = number.ToString( );
        int[] asArray = new int[asString.Length];
        for(int idx = 0; idx < asString.Length; idx++)
        {
            asArray[idx] =
Convert.ToInt32(asString[idx].ToString());
        }

        bool swapping = true;
        while( swapping )
        {
            swapping = false;
            for(int nIx = 0; nIx < asArray.Length - 1; nIx++)
            {
                if( asArray[nIx] > asArray[nIx + 1])
                {
                    int swapNumber = asArray[nIx];
                    asArray[nIx] = asArray[nIx + 1];
                    asArray[nIx + 1] = swapNumber;
                    swapping = true;
                }
            }
        }
        return asArray;
    }

    public static void Main()
    {
        int[] sortedNumbers = Digitize( 987654321 );
        foreach( int number in sortedNumbers )
        {
            Console.WriteLine( number );
        }
    }
}
```

> If you are using C# and want to use a number larger than **2147483647**, you will have to change the *asArray* array type and argument numbers type to a **long**. This is because the maximum **int32** value is **2147483647**. If you try to use anything larger than that, the compiler will say that the number is out of range.

The portion of the code we just added should look familiar; it is the same sort of solution for the bubble sort problem. We continue to loop during while(swapping) and for each one of those loops, we loop through the *asArray* and swap any values that need to be. When that is done, we then have the sorted *asArray* that we can return from the function.

This problem is a small step forward in how to use a couple different concepts to solve one issue. We also went into the basic tactics used to convert types into other types (called casting) in order to organize the data in a way we can reliable use during the sorting process.

Numbers As Words

Numbers to words is a common entry-level problem to solve. It is a sort of stepping stone from solely manipulating strings and solely manipulating numbers. It is also a fantastic problem regarding measuring your ability to break down what is going on and how to solve it.

Overview:

Write a function that translates an integer value into written words. As an example, it would translate 384 into "three hundred eight four".

> This problem is solved by starting small and working up. Don't let the "one trillion" intimidate you; it is completely solvable.

Rules:

- Does your function translate every number from 1 to 1,000,000,000,000?

> If you would like to try to solve this on your own, do so now. If you want to see the break down of the problem, go to the next page.

Numbers as Words solution

One of the interesting things about this problem is that it is usually given to those who have not been taught as basic way of solving it. This is a programming technique called recursion.

Recursion is the practice of having a function call itself, which is a bit of a head trip to begin to understand. To start to understand what is going on, there has to be a small discussion of some computer science.

A program consists of two types of memory usage: the heap and the stack. For the purposes of this problem and with recursion in mind, we only care about the stack. The stack is the memory the program uses during run time, or the memory that the program didn't know about using until your program told it to use it. This includes where the memory is stored when functions are called, as functions will duplicate data to manipulate them before returning those values back to the variables you declare in your program / those passed into the function.

Recursion uses the stack memory to duplicate the same function in different portions of memory as it calls itself. This means that for each time you call the same function within itself, that copy of the data in the function is different from the previous and if need be, the next.

To break this down a bit further, recursion is a bit like a while loop where the function will continue to call itself until a condition is met and then the stack begins to return values that were set during the previous version of the recursion all the way back down to the first call.

Now, how do we use this to solve the problem of numbers to words? Well, this is the cool bit:

Numbers to words is solved with one solution; meaning the way you convert 1 to "one" is the same as converting 1,000,000,000,000 to "one trillion". Let's start with a small number:

1234

Now, working from right to left in the number, read the numbers in the place of what value they represent and then replace it with 0.

```
1234 = 4
1230 = 30
1200 = 200
1000 = 1000
```

Now if you convert each of these numbers to their whole value, from last to first:

One thousand two hundred thirty four

Pretty cool huh? Recursion will help us here because we can get the whole value and then call the same function with what's remaining, which gives us the whole value from that, and then if needed, calls itself again, getting the whole value again, from the remainder of the previous.

```
"four" NumbersTwoWords( 1234 ) ->
    "Thirty" <- NumbersToWords( 1230 ) ->
        "Two hundred" <- NumbersToWords( 1200 ) ->
            "One thousand" <- NumbersToWords( 1000 )
```

Lets setup the functions:

We won't be using classes for this exercise and instead solve the problem with only a function. While using a class is an option, a function calling itself is the more literal practice of recursion. Otherwise, it would be a class creating the same class from within itself, which is effectively the same thing but more complicated than it needs to be.

JavaScript:

```javascript
function NumbersToWords( number ) {
    var toNineteen = { 1: "one",
                       2: "two",
                       3: "three",
                       4: "four",
                       5: "five",
                       6: "six",
                       7: "seven",
                       8: "eight",
                       9: "nine",
                       10: "ten",
                       11: "eleven",
                       12: "twelve",
                       13: "thirteen",
                       14: "fourteen",
                       15: "fifteen",
                       16: "sixteen",
                       17: "seventeen",
                       18: "eighteen",
                       19: "nineteen" };

    var tens       = { 20: "twenty",
                       30: "thirty",
                       40: "forty",
                       50: "fifty",
                       60: "sixty",
                       70: "seventy",
                       80: "eighty",
                       90: "ninety" };

    if( number <= 19 && number > 0 ) {

    } else if( number > 19 && number <= 99 ) {

    } else if( number >= 100 && number <= 999 ) {

    } else if( number >= 1000 && number <= 999999 ) {

    } else if( number >= 1000000 && number <= 999999999 ) {

    } else if( number >= 1000000000 && number <= 999999999999 ) {

    } else if( number == 1000000000000 ) {

    } else if( number > 0 ) {
        return "Out of range!";
    }
    return "";
}
```

Ruby:

```ruby
def NumbersToWords( number )
    toNineteen = { 1=> "one",
                   2=> "two",
                   3=> "three",
                   4=> "four",
                   5=> "five",
                   6=> "six",
                   7=> "seven",
                   8=> "eight",
                   9=> "nine",
                   10=> "ten",
                   11=> "eleven",
                   12=> "twelve",
                   13=> "thirteen",
                   14=> "fourteen",
                   15=> "fifteen",
                   16=> "sixteen",
                   17=> "seventeen",
                   18=> "eighteen",
                   19=> "nineteen" };

    tens       = { 20=> "twenty",
                   30=> "thirty",
                   40=> "fourty",
                   50=> "fifty",
                   60=> "sixty",
                   70=> "seventy",
                   80=> "eighty",
                   90=> "ninety" };

    if number <= 19 && number > 0

    elsif number > 19 && number <= 99

    elsif number >= 100 && number <= 999

    elsif number >= 1000 && number <= 999999

    elsif number >= 1000000 && number <= 999999999

    elsif number >= 1000000000 && number <= 999999999999

    elsif number == 1000000000000

    elsif number > 0
        return "Out of range!";
    end
    return "";
end
```

C#:

```csharp
public class Test
{
    public static string NumbersToWords( int number )
    {
        Hashtable toNineteen = new Hashtable( );
        toNineteen.Add( 1, "one" );
        toNineteen.Add( 2, "two" );
        toNineteen.Add( 3, "three" );
        toNineteen.Add( 4, "four" );
        toNineteen.Add( 5, "five" );
        toNineteen.Add( 6, "six" );
        toNineteen.Add( 7, "seven" );
        toNineteen.Add( 8, "eight" );
        toNineteen.Add( 9, "nine" );
        toNineteen.Add( 10, "ten" );
        toNineteen.Add( 11, "eleven" );
        toNineteen.Add( 12, "twelve" );
        toNineteen.Add( 13, "thirteen" );
        toNineteen.Add( 14, "fourteen" );
        toNineteen.Add( 15, "fifteen" );
        toNineteen.Add( 16, "sixteen" );
        toNineteen.Add( 17, "seventeen" );
        toNineteen.Add( 18, "eighteen" );
        toNineteen.Add( 19, "nineteen" );

        Hashtable tens = new Hashtable( );
        tens.Add( 20, "twenty" );
        tens.Add( 30, "thirty" );
        tens.Add( 40, "forty" );
        tens.Add( 50, "fifty" );
        tens.Add( 60, "sixty" );
        tens.Add( 70, "seventy" );
        tens.Add( 80, "eighty" );
        tens.Add( 90, "ninety" );

        if( number <= 19 && number > 0 )
        {

        }
        else if( number > 19 && number <= 99 )
        {

        }
        else if( number >= 100 && number <= 999 )
        {

        }
        else if( number >= 1000 && number <= 999999 )
        {

        }
        else if( number >= 1000000 && number <= 999999999 )
        {

        }
```

continued...

```
            else if( number >= 1000000000 && number <= 999999999999 )
            {

            }
            else if( number == 1000000000000 )
            {

            }
            else if( number > 0 )
            {
               return "Out of range!";
            }
            return "";
       }
   }
```

> C# USERS: Functions cannot exist outside a class in C#. The language is
> centered around everything being in an object but we don't have to use a
> custom class, we can use the default one on Codepad, or if you are using
> something else, the root of the program and use the main( ) function to call
> the function. Make sure to add static to the NumbersToWords function.

From this setup, we can calculate every possible number combination from 1 to one
trillion. The number being passed in needs to go through a series of conditions and when
one of them is true, we need to get the remainder of that number from the whole it
represents (the whole of 123 would be 100, with remainder of 23), and then pass the
remainder into a recursive function call of *NumbersToWords* so that can manage the result
and return us the string representing the word.

Let's add the logic to convert these numbers into their whole representations and start using recursion to calculate the remainders, resulting in the final product of converting a number into its word representation:

JavaScript:

```javascript
function NumbersToWords( number ) {
    var toNineteen = { 1: "one",
                       2: "two",
                       3: "three",
                       4: "four",
                       5: "five",
                       6: "six",
                       7: "seven",
                       8: "eight",
                       9: "nine",
                      10: "ten",
                      11: "eleven",
                      12: "twelve",
                      13: "thirteen",
                      14: "fourteen",
                      15: "fifteen",
                      16: "sixteen",
                      17: "seventeen",
                      18: "eighteen",
                      19: "nineteen" };

    var tens       = { 20: "twenty",
                       30: "thirty",
                       40: "fourty",
                       50: "fifty",
                       60: "sixty",
                       70: "seventy",
                       80: "eighty",
                       90: "ninety" };

    var remainder = 0;
    if( number <= 19 && number > 0 ) {
       return toNineteen[number];
    } else if( number > 19 && number <= 99 ) {
        remainder = number % 10;
        number -= remainder;
        return tens[number] + " " + NumbersToWords( remainder );
    } else if( number >= 100 && number <= 999 ) {
        remainder = number % 100;
        number -= remainder;
        return toNineteen[number / 100] + " hundred " +
NumbersToWords( remainder );
    }
    else if( number >= 1000 && number <= 999999 ) {
        remainder = number % 1000;
        number -= remainder;
        return NumbersToWords( number / 1000 ) + " thousand " +
NumbersToWords( remainder );
    }
```

continued...

```
    else if( number >= 1000000 && number <= 999999999 ) {
        remainder = number % 1000000;
        number -= remainder;
        return NumbersToWords( number / 1000000 ) + " million " +
NumbersToWords( remainder );
    } else if( number >= 1000000000 && number <= 999999999999 ) {
        remainder = number % 1000000000;
        number -= remainder;
        return NumbersToWords( number / 1000000000 ) + " billion "
+ NumbersToWords( remainder );
    } else if( number == 1000000000000 ) {
        return "one trillion";
    } else if( number > 0 ) {
        return "Out of range!";
    } else {
        return "";
    }
}

console.log( NumbersToWords( 134334462 ) );
```

Ruby:

```ruby
def NumbersToWords( number )
    toNineteen = { 1=> "one",
                   2=> "two",
                   3=> "three",
                   4=> "four",
                   5=> "five",
                   6=> "six",
                   7=> "seven",
                   8=> "eight",
                   9=> "nine",
                   10=> "ten",
                   11=> "eleven",
                   12=> "twelve",
                   13=> "thirteen",
                   14=> "fourteen",
                   15=> "fifteen",
                   16=> "sixteen",
                   17=> "seventeen",
                   18=> "eighteen",
                   19=> "nineteen" };

    tens       = { 20=> "twenty",
                   30=> "thirty",
                   40=> "fourty",
                   50=> "fifty",
                   60=> "sixty",
                   70=> "seventy",
                   80=> "eighty",
                   90=> "ninety" };

    remainder = 0
    if number <= 19 && number > 0
        return toNineteen.fetch( number )
    elsif number > 19 && number <= 99
        remainder = number % 10
        number -= remainder
        return tens.fetch( number ) + " " +
NumbersToWords( remainder )
    elsif number >= 100 && number <= 999
        remainder = number % 100
        number -= remainder
        return NumbersToWords( number / 100 ) + " hundred " +
NumbersToWords( remainder )
    elsif number >= 1000 && number <= 999999
        remainder = number % 1000
        number -= remainder
        return NumbersToWords( number / 1000 ) + " thousand " +
NumbersToWords( remainder )
    elsif number >= 1000000 && number <= 999999999
        remainder = number % 1000000
        number -= remainder
        return NumbersToWords( number / 1000000 ) + " million " +
NumbersToWords( remainder )
```

continued...

```
        elsif number >= 1000000000 && number <= 999999999999
            remainder = number % 1000000000
            number -= remainder
            return NumbersToWords( number / 1000000000 ) + " billion "
+ NumbersToWords( remainder )
        elsif number == 1000000000000
            return "one trillion"
        elsif number > 0
            return "Out of range!";
        end
        return "";
end

puts NumbersToWords( 134334462 )
```

C#:

```csharp
using System;
using System.Collections;

public class Test
{
    public static string NumbersToWords( int number )
    {
        Hashtable toNineteen = new Hashtable( );
        toNineteen.Add( 1, "one" );
        toNineteen.Add( 2, "two" );
        toNineteen.Add( 3, "three" );
        toNineteen.Add( 4, "four" );
        toNineteen.Add( 5, "five" );
        toNineteen.Add( 6, "six" );
        toNineteen.Add( 7, "seven" );
        toNineteen.Add( 8, "eight" );
        toNineteen.Add( 9, "nine" );
        toNineteen.Add( 10, "ten" );
        toNineteen.Add( 11, "eleven" );
        toNineteen.Add( 12, "twelve" );
        toNineteen.Add( 13, "thirteen" );
        toNineteen.Add( 14, "fourteen" );
        toNineteen.Add( 15, "fifteen" );
        toNineteen.Add( 16, "sixteen" );
        toNineteen.Add( 17, "seventeen" );
        toNineteen.Add( 18, "eighteen" );
        toNineteen.Add( 19, "nineteen" );

        Hashtable tens = new Hashtable( );
        tens.Add( 20, "twenty" );
        tens.Add( 30, "thirty" );
        tens.Add( 40, "forty" );
        tens.Add( 50, "fifty" );
        tens.Add( 60, "sixty" );
        tens.Add( 70, "seventy" );
        tens.Add( 80, "eighty" );
        tens.Add( 90, "ninety" );

        int remainder = 0;
        if( number <= 19 && number > 0 )
        {
            return (string)toNineteen[number];
        }
        else if( number > 19 && number <= 99 )
        {
            remainder = number % 10;
            number -= remainder;
            return (string)tens[number] + " " +
NumbersToWords( remainder );
        }
        else if( number >= 100 && number <= 999 )
        {
            remainder = number % 100;
            number -= remainder;
            return (string)toNineteen[number / 100] + " hundred " +
NumbersToWords( remainder );
        }
```

continued...

```
else if( number >= 1000 && number <= 999999 )
        {
            remainder = number % 1000;
            number -= remainder;
            return NumbersToWords( number / 1000 ) + " thousand " +
NumbersToWords( remainder );
        }
        else if( number >= 1000000 && number <= 999999999 )
        {
            remainder = number % 1000000;
            number -= remainder;
            return NumbersToWords( number / 1000000 ) + " million "
+ NumbersToWords( remainder );
        }
        else if( number >= 1000000000 && number <= 999999999999 )
        {
            remainder = number % 1000000000;
            number -= remainder;
            return NumbersToWords( number / 1000000000 ) + "
billion " + NumbersToWords( remainder );
        }
        else if( number == 1000000000000 )
        {
            return "one trillion";
        }
        else if( number > 0 )
        {
          return "Out of range!";
        }
        return "";
    }

    public static void Main()
    {
        Console.WriteLine( NumbersToWords( 134334462 ) );
    }
}
```

The first condition is the most simple, as we have a number for everything from 1 to 19 in our *toNineteen* hash table, so we just return that. In C#, we also have to cast the value into a string because like in the Scrabble Score test, values in the hash table for C# are objects, so we need to convert that into a string by casting it into a string.

Our second condition is the first time we have to use recursion as there is a remaining value to calculate. Let's say that number is 43. That means our whole number is 40 and our remainder is 3. 40 exists in our tens hash table and then when we use recursion, the call to *NumbersToWords* will return "three" from the *toNineteen* hash.

The third, forth, fifth, and fifth are the same. We get the remainder by dividing by what whole number the condition represents (100, 1000, 1000000, or 1000000000) and then subtract that from number, so we have the whole value that number represents. Then, this is where we begin to differ from the first and second condition, we return the result of *NumbersToWords* of the number divided by the whole number it represents. This number could be something above what *toNineteen* so we use *NumbersToWords* on the front half of the number as well as the second half.

To explain this a bit further, let's say the number is 123987. Because this is a number in the thousands, our remainder will be 987 and the whole value will be 123000. Because 123000 / 1000 = 123, we have to use this number in *NumbersToWords* to get what it represents and then add "thousand" to what's returned. Then, we get the value from 987 by again using *NumbersToWords*.

 Then we concatenate the word representation of that whole number ("hundred", "thousand", "million", "billion") and then concatenate the return of *NumbersToWords* with the argument being the remainder.

If the number is equal to 1000000000000, we simply return "one trillion". If the number is larger than that, we return, "Out of range!". Finally, if none of these conditions return anything, we return an empty string: ""; which only happens if the number being passed in is less than 0.

That's the whole problem. The interesting bit is that working out how to solve it is much more of an issue than actually writing the code to solve it. As you move forward as a programmer, this is often the case. You have to start to think of how to break these problems down and once you do, you realize that writing the code for it ends up being straight forward.

Conclusion

Programming is the knowledge of both the language you are using and the tools it offers, as well as the practice of using these tools. The cool thing with programming is that there are many ways of manipulating the data in just about anyway you'd like. All that takes is for you to write a lot of code and experiment with the results of what it is you're writing.

These problems are in no way a master class but they do set you on a path of what it takes to break down some everyday problems programmers face and a possible solution for them.

When it comes to practicing, there are a few websites that offer you thousands of different and unique problems:

www.codewars.com
www.coderbyte.com
www.codingame.com
www.hackerrank.com
www.leetcode.com

When it comes to being a working programmer, you have to write a lot of code, for a variety of problems. There is a range of usefulness when it comes to practice problems to everyday problems and what it takes to solve them. On top of that, the portion of the industry that you want to work in will have a completely different set of problems than any other. As an example, programming in the video games will be much different from programming in the web industry. Do your best to explore and keep an open mind on what is fun. Who knows, maybe you'll love writing code in a portion of the industry that you'd never think about working in prior.

Notes